Fant‹

Fallacies

and Where

to Find Them

David Robert Worley

First Published 2020

Independently Published

Paperback ISBN: 9798642868942

Second Edition

Typeset in Leelawadee UI

Find out more from the author at www.worleyDR.com

This book is dedicated to all of those who are struggling to articulate themselves, to those who are suppressed by religion and to all those who are sadly no longer with us - punished for being able to think for themselves.

A thank you to all my Patrons who continue to allow me to do the work I do.

Activism requires time; time typically spent working a full-time job.

It is vitally important that we, the content creators, get the chance to spend as much time as possible helping others with our content.

To do this, we rely on donations from people like you to keep the lights on.

If you would like to become a Patron for as little as $1 a month, please visit:

www.patreon.com/davidworley

Prologue

There are reasons why we accept ideas. These reasons are called our epistemology. Bad reasons for accepting ideas are extremely common and are referred to as logical fallacies. These flaws in logic permeate across all ideas but do not, by definition, invalidate a conclusion. It's just a bad reason for believing something. Claiming that you think cars are dangerous because the stars align in a particular way would not be a good reason for believing the claim. Despite the flawed reasoning, the conclusion is still correct. Nevertheless, it should be supported by statistics on car-related accidents, injuries, and deaths, while ignoring astrology.

Street epistemologists engage in conversations with strangers in a brief five-minute encounter. They try to get their conversation partner to consider the reasons behind their beliefs. Firstly, a good street epistemologist allows others to approach them. They are not there to evangelise or preach their ideas onto others. Once they agree to have a conversation, they decide on a topic that the interviewee believes and would feel comfortable discussing on camera. Topics can vary, ranging from belief in gods, ghosts, and aliens to conspiracy theories, morality, and political ideologies. It's essential to clarify what it is that they believe and accurately portray what their belief is throughout the conversation. Being able to demonstrate an understanding of their ideas builds trust between the interviewer and the interviewee. Street epistemologists make notes as the conversation progresses to ensure that their conversation partner's views are accurately portrayed. Initial questions include how confident they are in their belief and how they came to the conclusions that they currently hold. People often come to conclusions too quickly or don't properly analyse all of the available perspectives. If they did, their opinion might change. We sometimes hold on to ideas because they carry sentimental value, or because we trust the people who told us. We also get coerced into believing some of our thoughts from a young age. Towards the end of the discussion, they get asked if their confidence on the subject has changed. It's vital to know how to falsify a belief. Meaning, if you hold an opinion which can't be proven false, then there are no reasons to keep believing it.

When engaging in a conversation with someone regarding their beliefs, I recommend following Daniel Dennett's reformulation of Rapoport's Rules as a basis for engaging in honest and respectful dialogue. The rules are as follows:

1. Repeat their position back to them accurately
2. State what you agree on
3. State anything that you have learned
4. Respectfully criticise the argument

When stating their position back to them, you are proving that you understand the concept that you aim to challenge. Preferably, you should simplify their opinion so succinctly that they will thank you for explaining it in a way that was easy to understand. Knowing where you agree bolsters your rapport with them, especially if you can agree on points that aren't commonly agreed upon. Step 3 can be tricky. Expressing what you have learned from the other person can be interpreted as support for their position. This is why we clarify after step 2 that we will first state where we agree, and then where we disagree. You could go back and forth in the conversation by explaining one thing you agree on, and one thing you disagree on. Rapoport's Rules are challenging to stick to in reality, especially when others resort to some of the fallacies mentioned in this publication.

Think of ideas like islands. To travel from one idea to another, you need bridges. Golden Bridges, outlined in Peter Boghossian and James Lindsay's 'How to Have Impossible Conversations', are bridges that allow someone to travel from one idea to another without stigma. Stigmas can include comments such as 'You took your time! (to change your opinion)'. If we come across as self-righteous, arrogant, intolerant, dismissive, or unpleasant in any way, it becomes harder for people to *want* to listen to us. Unfortunately, we have to be liked to be heard, so be kind. Only explain concepts to people if they ask you to. Do not force information on people. Model the behaviour you wish to see in others.

This book aims to give you an understanding of flawed reasoning so that you can notice it in your future conversations. It becomes a lot easier to have healthier dialogues with people once you can respectfully articulate where they went wrong in their reasoning. Note, you should also be applying these fallacies to your arguments as we go along. You should be criticising your ideas far more than anyone else's. Who are you to judge someone for their faulty logic if you rely on poor reasoning yourself? As such, this book aims to be a whistle-stop tour of logical fallacies, explaining what they are, a few examples, and maybe a suggestion or two on how to counter them. There is a religious slant on this book. However, these concepts can be used to understand flaws in reasoning for a wide range of beliefs, not just gods.

The answers I have provided are for anyone who doesn't know how to identify these fallacies and subsequently wishes to respond to them. They are better suited to a calm discussion format with friends or family, rather than a professional debate. They are meant to be as concise as possible, not a final 'Checkmate' moment, as all discussions should be geared towards encouraging further discussions. If you have both agreed to a formal debate where both interlocutors are trying to win, you need to define what qualifies as winning first. One way to do this would be to compare the audience's views before and after the debate.

As you read this book, I hope you have an epiphany and realise that you use a particular fallacy all the time. I, by no means, claim that this is an exhaustive list, nor do I claim to go into as much detail as I could. Instead, this book is a gentle introduction to fallacies, much like dipping your toe in the water. If you have ever struggled to find the right words, then I hope this book helps you to hold your own. One of the most liberating things you can do for yourself is to gain a mastery of your language. Use it to help others understand where they went wrong, and be the positive force you want to see in the world.

Fantastic Fallacies

Strawman

Misrepresenting an argument as weaker than it is

Ad Hominem

Undermining someone's argument because of their character

Ad Populum

Claiming something is true because most people believe it

False Dichotomy

Proposing that there are only two options, usually polarised opposites

Circular Reasoning

Using a conclusion as part of the claim

Red Herring

Using a distraction to avoid answering the question

No True Scotsman

A person isn't a true believer because they fail a purity test

Cherry Picking

Only using data that supports the claim

Non Sequitur

Linking statements together that do not logically follow one another

Anecdotal Fallacy

Justifying a claim with personal experience

Appeal to Nature

Claiming something is good for you because it's natural

Preaching to the Choir

Proposing an argument to people who already agree

Appeal to Authority

Claiming that an authority's support validates the conclusion

Personal Incredulity

The argument is wrong because I don't understand it

False Equivalence

Sharing a trait makes 2 things the same

Appeal to Emotion

Trying to guilt trip someone into accepting a claim

Appeal to Tradition

Claiming something is right because it has always been done that way

Cognitive Dissonance

Believing two opposing ideas at the same time

Placebo Effect

Believing something can have an effect when it can't

Loaded Question

A question that contains an assumption

Sunk Cost

Holding on to an idea because it has cost you something

Gambler's Fallacy

Believing that luck is on your side

Ad Victoria

Putting emphasis on trying to beat your opponent

Danth's Law

Insisting that you have won an argument

Ad Baculum

Using force to promote the acceptance of a conclusion

Argument by Assertion

Asserting a claim despite contradicting evidence

Pascal's Wager

Believing a false dominant game strategy

Hasty Generalisation

A rushed conclusion based on insufficient evidence

Countdown Fallacy

Not giving another person enough time to respond

Appeal to Volume

Overcompensating by getting louder

Appeal to Faith

Basing a conclusion on zero evidence

Grandstanding

Seeking to impress the crowd

Tu Quoque

Claiming an action is justified because the accuser is a hypocrite

Projecting

Blaming other people for your behaviour

Slippery Slope

Assuming a specific action will lead to a negative chain of events

Ambiguity

Hiding true meaning with vague language

Anchoring

Overvaluing an initial piece of information

Composition (Division)

If a trait is true for the part (whole), then it's true for the whole (part)

Nut Picking

Representing an extreme opinion as the opinion of the whole group

Gaslighting

Attempting to make someone doubt their recollection of events

The Curse of Knowledge

Assuming knowledge is shared

Genetic Fallacy

Judging an argument based on its source

Argument from Ignorance

Claiming something is true because it has not yet been proven false

Middle Ground Fallacy

Assuming the right answer will always be halfway between two polarised options

Apophasis

Denying you're bringing up a subject when you are

Special Pleading

Making an exemption for yourself but not others

Halo Effect

You judge an idea depending on how much you like the speaker

Texas Sharpshooter

Identifying a pattern to fit your pre-existing opinion

Appeal to Motive

Dismissing a claim due to questionable incentives

The Fallacy Fallacy

Assuming a conclusion is wrong because a fallacy was used to justify it

Where to Find Them

Strawman

Misrepresenting an argument as weaker than it is

This is one of the most common fallacies you have probably heard of. The point of a Strawman in real life is that it gets put in a field to represent a person that isn't real. Similarly, this fallacy places a weaker argument in front of an audience and presents it as if it were your actual position. If someone misrepresents your opinion, let them know. Do not proceed with the conversation until they can accurately state your idea back to you. Claiming, "Evolution states that chimps give birth to humans" is a bit like saying, "Christians believe we all came from talking snakes". Both are similar portrayals of the real arguments, but both are dishonest misrepresentations of Evolution and Genesis, respectively. If you want to be taken seriously, take a genuine interest in your interlocutor's actual opinion. Follow Rapoport's Rules, and build a solid foundation upon which you can both proceed with a respectful and dignified conversation.

Ad Hominem

Undermining someone's argument because of their character

This isn't just attacking someone with insults like, "You're stupid", rather it implies that they are wrong as a result, by saying, "You're wrong because you're stupid". As soon as you start claiming that someone is wrong because of *who* they are, you lose focus on the real issue of *what* they are saying. Always focus on the argument and not the person. This is advised even if they are engaging with you in an aggressive or demeaning manner. An Ad Hominem can take multiple forms, from simple insults to full-scale misrepresentations of someone's character. It is usually used as a method of distraction when they don't have a suitable reply but feel the need to react quickly. An excellent example of this is saying that 'Atheists are the devil', absolving any responsibility to take genuine objections to morality in the Bible seriously. Instead, encourage them to spend more time formulating their thoughts, and get back to you once they have a suitable response.

Ad Populum

Claiming something is true because most people believe it

Arguments like these usually sound like, "How can X number of people be wrong?" People who are isolated from opposing ideas are susceptible to this fallacy. Their worldview is warped by the fact that they perceive other opinions outside of their group as minority opinions. Just because there are 2 billion Christians in the world, doesn't mean they are right. By definition, a majority disagrees with that opinion, that doesn't mean that the position is wrong. Following this argument to its logical conclusion, no claim can be true until at least 50% of people agree with it. Ask how many people need to agree with the position for it to be considered correct. If they have the majority in the room agreeing with them, would it be just as logical to assume that the opposite is true if the whole town disagrees? By what criteria did they reject the opinions of those outside of the room? Does the number of adherents to an idea affect whether a claim is valid?

False Dichotomy

Proposing that there are only two options, usually polarised opposites

Either you are with me or against me. If you're not good, you're evil. If you didn't vote for my candidate, you must be dumb. Scientists don't know everything, therefore God. If you're not willing to have sex with trans people, then you are transphobic. Ask yourself if there any other options. Is this a situation where a closed yes or no answer is acceptable, or is there nuance to discuss? The polarisation of modern-day discussion has led to people being scared to talk about sensitive topics without being dismissed as extreme. It is vital for the health of our conversations that we stop misrepresenting those with different opinions as having an extreme perspective. The only way we can resolve disputes with civility is to engage in honest discourse. We must nurture an understanding that the person we are talking to is, at worst, misguided. It is advised to give maximal charity to others when they speak, assuming only honest intentions from the beginning.

Circular Reasoning

Using a conclusion as part of the claim

Tricky to notice, this fallacy contains the conclusion within one of its premises. Also called Begging the Question, this fallacy assumes the conclusion before a proper analysis is even attempted. If we ask a fundamentalist Muslim why they believe the Quran, they might say, "because it's infallible". When asked why they think that it's infallible, they might say, "It's the word of Allah". They accept that because "It says so in the Quran". Ask them if this logic applies to other gods. Play devil's advocate, if you will. Come up with alternative examples of the fallacy to test their understanding of it. Ask them to identify where the sentence, "This country is the best in the world because it's just so great" or "I have the right to own a gun because it's legal" goes wrong. Whenever someone claims that 'there is no better argument for the existence of a God than the truth of their existence', remember, this book is infallible because it's the word of Dave. How do I know that? It says so in this book... which is infallible.

Red Herring

Using a distraction to avoid answering the question

Used often by politicians, this is used when they want to avoid criticism. When the Catholic church receives criticism for the sexual abuse of children, their defenders will point to how much good work the Catholic church has done for charity, as if this in some way negates the harm. They may claim that without the church, so many good things would not have happened. The church should be held accountable for their actions no matter how much good they may have done elsewhere. Keep focus and hold an authority to account. Switch to closed yes / no questions to get a straight answer out of anyone who tries to avoid answering the question. If they still resist, ask them to ask you the same question. Answer it immediately. Then, ask the same question again. This technique is called modelling, or in other words, demonstrating the behaviour that you wish to see in others. Use it often, but allow others enough time to properly consider their answer.

No True Scotsman

A person isn't a true believer because they fail a purity test

"Only a real Scotsman would be able to down a bottle of Whisky in 10 seconds" is fallacious. A Scotsman is defined as those that are born in Scotland and not by how much they can drink or how quickly. Some Christians will claim that other Christians are not real Christians if they accept gay marriage, or are part of a different denomination like the Seventh Day Adventists. They don't get to decide who is a real Christian, as they are not the gatekeeper of who is or isn't a proper believer. The argument could just as easily be used against them, by someone who defines their version of Christianity as substandard. This claim starts with a general principle such as, "All Christians follow the King James Bible" and then when other versions of the Bible are put forward, the No True Scotsman fallacy is proposed instead of retracting their original, now discredited, statement. Avoid making any vague, general statements in the future.

Cherry Picking

Only using data that supports the claim

The name is derived from the idea that only cherries that are ripe enough to be sold for a profit will be harvested. The rest of the cherries will be ignored until they become ripe for picking. Those that claim that all morality comes from the Bible will be Cherry Picking. In Exodus 21:24, it states 'eye for an eye', about justice. Later, in Matthew 5:39, it says to 'turn to them the other cheek' about mercy. Many passages of the Bible contradict each other, so you have to choose which morals you take from it. We could do several surveys on whether people like their world leaders. Each survey asked 100 people what they thought, and 4 out of 5 surveys said they hated them. The world leader then points to the fifth survey and declares that they are popular when, in reality, a more significant number of people said they hated them. Ask 'is the data put forward representative of the whole data set, or only some of it? Is there data being kept hidden to propagate a specific narrative?'

Non Sequitur

Linking statements together that do not logically follow one another

Exceptionally tricky to notice, the Non Sequitur usually contains several truths. A simple example would be:

1. Fish can swim
2. Dave can swim
3. Therefore, Dave is a fish

Users will state some truths, and smuggle in a lie or an assumption that does not logically follow from the previous statements. As a remedy, take things slow, write down their syllogism if you must, and determine if each sentence makes sense. You can also make a Non Sequitur argument out of just truths, so question them on how they know that the previous statements link into the latter. Check for sources. Theists can use this fallacy to justify anything, such as, "God says giving to the poor is good, the church wants to help the poor; therefore, you should tithe 10% of your wages to the church".

Anecdotal Fallacy

Justifying a claim with personal experience

There are two types of anecdotal fallacy; an experience you had, and an experience you believe someone else had. It's harder to prove someone else's experience than your own. Other people's experiences are believable if you trust the storyteller, almost like a Halo Effect. This does not necessarily make a claim right. If it's your anecdote, check for other people that have had similar experiences. Note their similarities and differences. If someone has a belief based on anecdotal evidence, ask what happened, where, when, and how. Is it possible that their anecdote could have been mistaken? If they can be mistaken, can you? If the anecdote involved their God, why has no one ever believed a story that involved a god they had never previously heard of? The Police will not trust recall memory as it's known to be an inaccurate source of evidence. Keep asking them pointed, specific questions. Is their story consistent?

Appeal to Nature

Claiming something is good for you because it's natural

Usually used in commercials for beauty products, debates on abortion, or home-made medicines, Appeals to Nature need to be carefully administered. Nobody would think in their right mind that Uranium is good for you, just because it's natural. Find out how they define 'natural', and why they believe one option is better than the other. They are likely to distrust synthetic, man-made products. Ask them if they think that unnatural things are bad for you and why. How do they define 'unnatural'? Homeopathic remedies are watered-down medicines that only dilute the effectiveness of the real drug. The doctors prescribing such 'cures' are seeking to make a quick profit off of you by putting your health at risk. Pro-lifers might be getting their views on abortion from their religion. If their God doesn't come from nature, but rather, their God created it, then is God bad for us, if only natural things are good?

Preaching to the Choir

Proposing an argument to people who already agree

This technique is used to further cement an opinion that people have already accepted, or minimise dissent from those who are questioning. Similar to seeking consensus with an Ad Populum, 'Preaching to the Choir' involves the reinforcement of established ideas, rather than trying to convert non-believers. Political rallies serve as platforms to rile up believers and get them to be more active campaigners. The problem is that this fallacy often creates an echo chamber, where alternative ideas aren't even considered, and reinforcement of existing ideas is compulsory. Instead, we should be encouraged to discover all possible opinions to find out which ones are best, not just accepting our pre-existing ideology. Ask them how well they can articulate other people's views who disagree with their own, as per rule 1 of Rapoport's Rules. Usually, simple exposure to different ideas can go a long way to winning over a potential convert.

Appeal to Authority

Claiming that an authority's support validates the conclusion

There is nothing wrong with saying that an expert in their chosen field knows more than you do. The problem is claiming someone is an authority in a chosen field when they are not. The wording may feel pedantic, but it's important to say that you believe in something because the data heavily implies a strong likelihood that it is true, rather than suggesting that the people who collated the data are to be believed. Beware of experts who stray out of their chosen field, but also guard against those who claim that they are free from scrutiny because they have higher qualifications than you, especially if they got their doctorate in a bogus field of study, or from a diploma mill. Trusting your doctor is not the same as an appeal to authority. They are experts who have studied their field for many years. It would be fallacious to take a politician's opinion on healthcare during a global pandemic to determine how to treat it, as their politics are irrelevant to curing it.

Personal Incredulity

The argument is wrong because I don't understand it

Some ideas take longer than others to properly comprehend. Anyone who is sincerely trying to achieve rule 1 of Rapoport's Rules deserves recognition for doing so. The problem lies with those who do not bother to try. If people want to understand a perspective, but don't, be patient with them. If someone dismisses an idea because they don't understand it, it may be that your presentation of the concept may be challenging for them to understand. Remember that some people are more visual learners than others, or they may prefer to read. They may understand better if you use an equivalence or a similarly framed argument. Anyone who is being particularly challenging to get through to may find it beneficial to have their arguments rejected by you, using the same logic they used to reject yours. See if they accept the example "Your beliefs are so unbelievable that it can't be true".

False Equivalence

Sharing a trait makes 2 things the same

When proposing an equivalence, it is recommended to stick to the same field of study. An equivalence is an argument that compares two things that share a trait. The trait in question determines whether or not the equivocation being made is a sound one. For example, it could be argued that "the killing of animals in the meat industry is like a 21st-century holocaust". They are similar, in that they both involve millions of deaths. The equivocation stops when we realise that Jews in World War 2 were not slaughtered to be eaten, but were erased, as they were deemed inferior by far-right ideologues. This is not to be confused with a False Analogy, in which trait A is shared; therefore, they also share trait B. Instead, a False Equivalence is best understood as sharing trait A; therefore, they are the same. Question the fact that Jesus and Hitler both had facial hair. That doesn't mean that they are the same. The trait they share is irrelevant.

Appeal to Emotion

Trying to guilt trip someone into accepting a claim

'You have to give me the job. My child depends on me, and I don't want to be left out on the streets!' The candidate in question has no discernible skills that the job requires, and as such, there is no logical reason to employ them. The use of emotion here is used to manipulate the situation in their favour. This is not to be confused with stating a sound logical syllogism passionately. An Appeal to Emotion replaces a rational argument with emotion when no sound reason is proposed. The most significant Appeal to Emotion of all time has to be the concept of hell. The fear of hell is so intense that many an atheist or apostate have claimed to still fear it after their deconversion, even though they have already accepted that there is no logical reason to believe in it. Animal rights activists have used blood-stained images for years to provoke a visceral response in people, while not putting nearly as much effort into making the moral argument.

Appeal to Tradition

Claiming something is right because it has always been done that way

Some traditions are worth keeping. The problem is when you do something for no other reason but tradition. It is often used as a means to avoid updating methods with the times. New technology brings improvement but also risks if it doesn't work, teething problems in its infancy, or it might be too expensive to implement at the time. It may be that these are perfectly non-fallacious reasons for not modernising. An Appeal to Tradition is often used as a way for theists to dismiss gay marriage activists and human rights advocates, as their views are not deemed proper. Think of it as a No True Scotsman fallacy for morals rather than people or groups. Would it be rational for slave owners to defend the ownership of slaves because 'We have always had slaves'? Ask for any sound, logical reasons outside of tradition that prop up their perspective, and suggest that these reasons should be sufficient enough to uphold their claims.

Cognitive Dissonance

Believing two opposing ideas at the same time

This is when actions do not correlate with beliefs. It sounds counter-intuitive, and that's because it is. Be that as it may, it's common to hold opposing ideas. Many people who smoke know it will kill them. Many Christians disagree with slavery, misogyny, incest, homophobia, and genocide, but still claim the Bible to be their source of morality. Buyer's Remorse is trying to convince yourself you made a good purchase when in reality you want to return the item. This is usually countered by internalising one's thoughts about many subjects. Ask "Am I pretending to hold a position because the pay-off is worth it" or "If I reject an idea, why haven't I changed my behaviour?" Identify if the idea in question is comforting or reasonable. There must be another underlying reason why they have not changed their behaviour yet. Sometimes, someone doesn't realise they hold opposing ideas. Be kind.

Placebo Effect

Believing something can have an effect when it can't

Homeopathic drugs are watered down medicines that make you think you're getting better when you aren't. If you get better anyway, you may have attributed your recovery to the Placebo Effect, rather than just getting better due to your immune system. It is essentially attempting to think your problem away. James Randi, stage magician, would regularly take a whole bottle of homeopathic pills at the start of his shows, much to the bemusement of his audience. Later, he explains what the drugs are, demonstrating that you cannot overdose from them because the medicine is so diluted. Conmen will sell their products to make a profit, rather than curing you of anything. Prayer works in the same way. You can test how praying to different gods results in similar success rates. If you think someone you know is being sold a placebo, encourage them to stop spending their money on miracle cures.

Loaded Question

A question that contains an assumption

Have you ever been asked a question that has made you take a step back and think, "Wait... that's not right", but didn't know how to respond? Trick questions invoke Morton's Fork, a technique designed to result in multiple guilty answers, no matter how you respond. Once you become aware of the Loaded Question, you realise how common it is. If I ask, "Why do you hate God", I am assuming you hate them. This is the second question of two. The first question is, "Do you hate God?" Skipping the first question - because they assume the answer – results in misunderstanding. Be careful answering these questions, as answering them will sometimes be interpreted as admitting to the assumptions mentioned above. To avoid this, state very clearly, "That's a Loaded Question". If they ask what that means, explain what they have assumed. Only continue the conversation once they can accurately state your position as per Rule 1 of Rapoport's Rules.

Sunk Cost

Holding on to an idea because it has cost you something

Used when people want to recover previous losses by continuing an act, it is often a denial that is difficult to admit without some form of expected stigma. This is not to be confused with the Argument from Inertia, in which you refuse to stop doing something because you would have to admit personal responsibility. A Sunk Cost pertains to the time, money, and resources involved being lost. This fallacy is often credited to describing gamblers who can't walk away from a game. If they did, they would have to admit to the losses they have already made. Apostates, those that have left religion, often cite that they experienced a great deal of pushback for their decision, but ultimately made the right choice. The Sunk Cost Fallacy is often perceived to be a barrier for apostates. Leaving would be an admittance that they have wasted a great deal of time and money.

Gambler's Fallacy

Believing that luck is on your side

When playing Roulette, gambler's that see a run of consecutive results, like 5 black numbers in a row, feel like the next number is more likely to be a red. In truth, each spin of the wheel is independent of each other. The Gambler's Fallacy is the expectation that the odds of an event happening are increasing on an exponential curve. Over time, we expect our chances of winning to rise, when, in fact, they don't change. This expectation that the world evens itself out can lead to beliefs in karma or justice paradigms. Believers in heaven and hell expect unfair results on Earth to be 'corrected'. This is partly due to our nature as pattern seekers. Those that believe that luck is on their side are susceptible to the Sunk Cost fallacy. The Reverse Gambler's Fallacy suggests that because we have seen success in the past, we are now more likely to see success in the future. This fallacy is worsened when people tend to believe their God can alter a result in their favour.

Ad Victoria

Putting emphasis on trying to beat your opponent

This is the first of a couple of fallacies I have named myself. Before you engage in a conversation, especially a debate, it's advised to outline in your opening remarks that you value learning other people's perspectives. Aim to avoid misrepresenting your conversation partner's opinion during the discussion. There is real value in highlighting someone else's mistakes from a position of respect. Make your intentions clear from the get-go. Be transparent. Admit if you are trying to impress them, educate them, or embarrass them. If you go into a discussion to beat them, there is a greater tendency towards losing their respect and misrepresenting what they are saying (Strawman), reciting practised putdowns (Grandstanding), and engaging in a popularity contest (Ad Populum). If someone does this, immediately remind them that these fallacies do nothing to strengthen their argument.

Danth's Law

Insisting that you have won an argument

If you have to insist that you won, you probably didn't. This all goes back to outlining what you want to achieve in a discussion. In some cases, it is justified to declare yourself the victor. Because this fallacy happens after the debate, it is essential to timestamp the exact moments that they thought won them the argument. It is more likely that they will ignore discrepancies in their arguments and declare by fiat that they were better, no matter how well the debate went. In this case of defiance, ask them, "Was it possible for you to lose? What would losing look like? What does your opponent need to do in the future to beat you?" If they had determined that they were going to win before the debate even happened, they have committed an A Priori fallacy. Ask them at what moment they thought they had won the debate, and if they can accurately explain their opponent's position. As a victor, surely it would be easy to articulate the opinion they're refuting.

Ad Baculum

Using force to promote the acceptance of a conclusion

Surah 4:34 is often quoted as a verse in the Quran used to justify the beating of women if their husbands *fear* their dissent. People tend to resort to violence as a way of scaring people into subordination, instead of having a sound, reasonable argument. This can often be a traumatic experience for victims that lasts for a long time, leaving them to look over their shoulder in fear during normal everyday activities. Anyone engaging in force to promote their ideology needs to be reported to the relevant authorities immediately. This isn't always easy in certain parts of the world. Theocracies don't always take the word of a victim seriously, especially given that Surah 2:282 dictates that the testimony of a woman is worth half that of a man. Using such force against children, to coerce them into a religion out of fear, is obscene. Seek local secular groups that can help you - or someone you know - out of an abusive situation.

Argument by Assertion

Asserting a claim despite contradicting evidence

This is characterised by being stubborn in the face of a sound, reasonable rebuttal. You can claim arguments as true or false by assertion. Repetition of the same statement in the hope that it will wear down the opponent might work on children but is not a valid reason to believe anything. Cult leaders use this to seek obedience from their followers. The epitome of brainwashing, the best way to deal with this fallacy is to highlight the fact that they are only making a claim, rather than backing it up with evidence. If they assert something is right, question why they believe it by asking them for their epistemology, the reasons why they think it's true. They may claim, "I know because I know", in which case, you can respond by asserting an opposing claim by the same logic. When they ask you how you know, state, "I know because I know". Their answer as to why they haven't accepted your argument is the same reason why you don't accept theirs.

Pascal's Wager

Believing a false dominant game strategy

This argument compares the benefits of believing and not believing in an afterlife, like so:

1) I believe in God, and they are real = heaven
2) I believe in God, and they aren't real = 0
3) I don't believe, and they are real = hell
4) I don't believe, and they aren't real = 0

It implies that you're better off hedging your bets on God. However, it's not clear which God. The model assumes the afterlife and doesn't consider other versions of heaven or hell. If one version of hell is the worst, should we convert to that religion? The wager is an over-simplified version of reality, seen as a selfish attempt to trick an all-knowing god into absolving you of responsibility for your actions. Pascal's Wager can be used as evidence for accepting any god. Ask them why they don't accept a different one. Consider Worley's Wager - Climate Change is real, using Pascal's Wager.

Hasty Generalisation

A rushed conclusion based on insufficient evidence

People will rush to a conclusion if they have already predetermined the answer before they have even tried to find the evidence to prove it. These people run the risk of Confirmation Bias, where they attempt to find only the sources that support their pre-existing beliefs. They are likely to have only considered a small amount of data before they reached their conclusion. Test their conclusion by asking, "Have you considered all of the available data? Can this be applied to other groups?" Some atheists, like Stalin, have committed atrocities. It would be fallacious to assume that this means that all atheists are dangerous, or people with moustaches cannot be trusted. This fallacy is common amongst conspiracy theorists and those who do not make a sincere attempt to understand other people's beliefs. Those who wish to confirm their pre-existing ideology through Confirmation Bias will find a way to do so.

Countdown Fallacy

Not giving another person enough time to respond

The second fallacy that I have named myself is simply not giving someone enough time to respond. If you hesitate, stutter, or fail to react quickly enough, it is deemed enough - by a dishonest interlocutor - to claim victory and jump headfirst into Danth's Law. If you need a moment to compose your answer, say, "Please give me a moment to gather my thoughts. I'm trying to figure out how to respond to that in the most effective way." If they insist on a quick answer, do not proceed until you find out why they are being so pushy. Ask them, "What happens if I take longer to respond with a more accurate answer?" Some debaters will agree to written debates with word limits that span many months. Offer to have a written discussion with someone if the topic at hand is too contentious to discuss face to face. This way, the problem doesn't seep its way into everyday conversation and interfere with family gatherings or the like.

Appeal to Volume

Overcompensating by getting louder

This should be obvious, but do not rise to the challenge of getting louder. Petulant children do this when they don't get what they want, and can only lead to you being interpreted as one. The key here is to remember to lower your volume when they raise theirs. Make them realise that *they* are ones losing control. Be clear and concise with your message and do not back down. Speak slower, but do not sound patronising. Behave like a parent would towards a toddler having a tantrum. Model the behaviour you wish to see in others. If this happens amongst family members, or happens with someone you know personally, you may feel compelled to back down for the sake of your relationship (Appeasement). To sustain your relationship, but also stand firm in your opinions, offer the aforementioned written debate format. Agree to a word or page limit, and clarify that there is no rush to reply. This way, contentious conversations do not seep into everyday life.

Appeal to Faith

Basing a conclusion on zero evidence

Usually, someone who uses an Appeal to Faith doesn't apply their reasoning to other people's beliefs. Every religion will claim that they are right, based on faith. Only a maximum of one of them can be true. The reason '...because it's my faith' cannot be used to justify the truth, as faith can lead to multiple conclusions. Ask them, "Is there any opinion that can't be believed based on faith?" This question forces your conversation partner to consider other beliefs. The main reason they give for their belief is a reason that supports every idea. If someone has a particularly controversial view based on faith, you can demonstrate that the complete opposite view can also be claimed based on the same argument. Joke gods like the Flying Spaghetti Monster can be believed based on faith, but that doesn't make it real. As the late, great Christopher Hitchens once said - "It's called faith, because it's not knowledge".

Grandstanding

Seeking to impress the crowd

When you try to provoke a reaction from the audience, typically support, you are grandstanding. This distracts from the discussion at hand and tries to capitalise on a temporary advantage in crowd numbers. Done right, grandstanding requires sharp wit, quick thinking, and a mastery of the subject at hand. However, in the wrong hands, it can be a cheap attempt to ridicule your opponent, makes your conversation partner feel uncomfortable, and is transparent. This can be followed by an Ad Populum, where a user claims to be right because the majority agrees with them. This is different from claiming, "the data suggests my conclusion, and it just so happens that the crowd is also on my side". State that they are Grandstanding to gain a favourable opinion from their audience. Ask anyone engaging in this fallacy if their argument is strengthened by Grandstanding. Rein them back towards the topic of the discussion using closed questions to get a straight answer out of them.

Tu Quoque

Claiming an action is justified because the accuser is a hypocrite

Tu Quoque means 'you also' in Latin. It is the attempt to legitimise your actions by pointing towards your accuser, who does the same thing. If 2 people have committed sexual assault, and the first person tries to call them out on it, the second person might turn around and say, "You're one to talk!" To be fair, the accuser *is* being a hypocrite, but that doesn't make them wrong. When referring to theist debates, someone might be accused of questionable morals or ethics. If a prominent member of the Catholic church is challenged over the sexual abuse of children by a Jehovah's Witness, they should have the decency to take responsibility and create safeguards to make sure it doesn't happen again. They would succumb to this fallacy if they were to respond with, "What about the sexual abuse of children in *your* church!" As we have already discovered, bad behaviour does not justify bad behaviour.

Projecting

Blaming other people for your behaviour

Similar to a Tu Quoque, Projecting is denying any wrongdoing while claiming other people have behaved that way instead. Shifting the blame to the innocent is common amongst bullies, of all ages, who insist on intimidation tactics and shouting over those perceived as weaker than them. If you're accused of wrongdoing by a Projector, calmly and bluntly deny the claim, then ask for their evidence. Highlight that this behaviour was, in fact, theirs. Refer to any evidence you have against them, frequently, preferably in video format, like a live interview. When you make your complaints publicly, people close to the Projector start to notice their awful behaviour and will begin to distance themselves from them. This may cause the Projector to double down and accuse you even more. Do not give them a chance to respond with threats - they will only try to intimidate you further. You can find out more about Dog Whistles in *Fantastic Fallacies and Brilliant Biases*.

Slippery Slope

Assuming a specific action will lead to a negative chain of events

There are some theists - who seem to sincerely believe - that if you become an atheist, you are devoid of morality and will start smoking, taking drugs, worshipping the devil, become a rapist, murder a bunch of people, and would be entirely ok with eating babies. Speaking as an atheist, and not on behalf of all other atheists, I have done none of those things. Break down why someone thinks that these events logically follow on from one another. Ask them, "What makes you think that will happen?" Find out why a simple action is expected to lead to more extreme consequences. When used vindictively, it can be used to scare children into conforming with expected behaviour, for fear of hell. If they make the argument that gay marriage will lead to infidelity (or some other effect deemed detrimental), you can demonstrate the Slippery Slope back at them. Suggest that banning gay marriage will lead to bans on all forms of marriage.

Ambiguity

Hiding true meaning with vague language

A deity, a.k.a. a creator god and nothing else, is a vague concept. Politicians use vague language all the time so that when they are caught out, they get to say, "well actually I meant..." to avoid criticism. It's a slippery and dishonest way to go about discourse. Use precise language. Get to the point. The Kalam Cosmological Argument appeals to Ambiguity. It states, "Everything that begins to exist has a cause, the universe began to exist; therefore, the universe had a cause, which is my God". The ambiguity here is that the term 'cause' does not necessarily mean 'create' - like comparing a bonfire being created and a wildfire during the dry season. Attributing agency to events where there are none is common, and could even be explained by evolution. Note that the Kalam does nothing to prove it's *their* God and implies their creator was also created. The ambiguity of the word 'nothing' when discussing the creation of the universe has caused significant disagreement.

Anchoring

Overvaluing an initial piece of information

If you were looking to sell a house, your first estate agent might evaluate it to be worth £500,000. You then proceed to only consider offers above that price, when other estate agents might evaluate it at its true worth of £400,000. With offers of £450,000 being rejected, your initial anchoring to the first offer has resulted in you missing out on selling your house for more than what it's worth. If an Apple product was released too cheaply, then it might not sell because of a perceived lack of quality. Holy books are used as anchors, in the same way, to convince children that God is real. Our first impressions are considered to be extremely important for this reason. In reality, there is insufficient data to be making such a Hasty Generalisation upon a person or a company's character. Always question whether you put your trust in a particular source for good reasons, rather than the first impression you got from them.

Composition (Division)

If a trait is true for the part (whole), then it's true for the whole (part)

If the best player in the world plays for your team, it does not logically follow that you have the best team in the world. This is Composition. It's highly popular with Flat Earthers, who would claim that because a glass of water appears flat on the surface, for them, the ocean must also be flat. Inversely, Division would assume that because my house is twice the size of yours, that means that the doors, windows, chairs, and everything else inside my house must be twice the size as well. Both sides of this fallacy assume that because one property is true for one thing, it must be true for other things too. Question the underlying evidence for making such a claim that you suspect to be in breach of this fallacy. Use examples like, "If we can't see atoms - and people are made of atoms - does that mean we can't see people?" or "The Bible supports slavery. Does that mean all Christians should support slavery?"

Nut Picking

Representing an extreme opinion as the opinion of the whole group

Nut Picking is essentially Guilt by Association, used to dismiss and ridicule a group as more bizarre than they are. The fallacy of Composition states 'if it's true for the part, it's true for the whole'. In contrast, Nut Picking is better defined as saying 'if it's true for the part, it's true for all other parts'. If I were to say that, "some Muslims are suicide bombers; therefore, all Muslims are suicide bombers", that's Nut Picking. If I said, "some Muslims are suicide bombers; therefore, Islamic countries are suicide bombers", that would be Composition (and nonsensical). Aptly named, this fallacy attempts to misrepresent the fringes as the mainstream, especially when it comes to differences in political opinion. The only reason to be concerned by a group with extreme views is if that group has a disproportionate number of members with extreme views, or attempts to promote those views. In other words, it's Cherry Picking a lunatic to Strawman an Ad Hominem attack.

Gaslighting

Attempting to make someone doubt their recollection of events

A manipulative way of deceiving someone, this is used by pick up artists and abusive partners to control their victim, who can be made to feel guilty for everything, more anxious, and less confident. A Gaslighter will use inconsistent arguments to make their partner question their reality. The signs of abuse can start small, making you question whether you had agreed to attend an event. As the manipulation progresses, they will start sentences with 'You think/want...' as they implant their ideas into your head. Then, they make it sound like you are backtracking on something you never agreed to, by undermining everything you say. As you doubt yourself more and more, they switch to bare-faced lies and making fun of you in front of your mutual friends, knowing the chances of you challenging them has dissolved. The only option for victims is to leave such an abusive relationship immediately. Seek therapy if necessary.

The Curse of Knowledge

Assuming knowledge is shared

When writing, it's important to simplify what we're trying to convey. We sometimes forget that not everyone knows the words we use, or what they mean. Epistemology (the reasons why we believe) or Theist (a believer in a God that can edit the universe) are such words. The curse typically happens when you attempt to engage in a conversation, but you forget to mention the build-up to that conversation you were just having inside your head. How many times have you heard a phrase as vague as 'Have you done it yet?' when clearly 'it' could relate to anything from mowing the lawn to doing your homework. A famous experiment was done by researchers, who asked participants to tap the tune to Happy Birthday on a table to see how quickly the other person could guess the song. Unsurprisingly, the tappers overestimated their abilities, as only 2% of guessers got the tune right. Be careful in assuming anything, and take a moment to clarify whether what you are about to say would make sense to a child.

Genetic Fallacy

Judging an argument based on its source

This is suggesting a claim either isn't true or at the very least is less acceptable, because of where it came from. You might feel justified in dismissing a source if they're consistently inaccurate on a subject, such as a preacher that refuses to correct their Strawman of Evolution. A specific media outlet may have been reporting factually inaccurate statements for years. When they do say something of genuine value or substance, it gets dismissed. A simple version of the fallacy would be, "I believe in God because my parents told me it's real". They can be wrong, and so the source should not be used as a foundation for the claim. A Genetic Fallacy tends to be more specific in where it comes from, like a holy book, a newspaper, or a company. Note that this fallacy can be used to bolster an argument and not just dismiss it. Claiming the belief is true because it came from your favourite source still counts as the Genetic Fallacy.

Argument from Ignorance

Claiming something is true because it has not yet been proven false

The basic form this takes is saying, "You can't disprove the claim; therefore, it must be true". The burden of proof lies solely on the person making a claim, not the one refuting it. If they cannot provide such evidence, it would be wise to reject the claim until such evidence becomes apparent. This tactic is almost an admittance that the user doesn't have sufficient evidence, but one should not assume such things until they are stated clearly. It is often used when someone doesn't have a better response at the time. Outline to them that any position can be taken if we rely on others to disprove our claims. Ask how they refuted a position opposite to theirs. Determine how to falsify each other's claim, i.e. what criteria do we need to stop believing in what we currently accept as true. Conversely, identify what would count as sufficient evidence to prove each other's claim, and work together to discover what meaningful evidence there is out there.

Middle Ground Fallacy

Assuming the right answer will always be halfway between two polarised options

If one side of an argument wants to get rid of nuclear weapons and the other half want to keep them, then keeping half the weapons will solve nothing. An aspect of this fallacy is that in accepting it, you tend to fall for another one. The Balance fallacy is when 2 people in a debate are treated as if their arguments have equal merit when they don't. Depolarising the conversation away from False Dichotomies can help. Identify a spectrum of opinions and analyse each of them carefully, rather than assume there are only 2 polarised perspectives and an optimal position halfway in between. The fallacy, in many respects, comes from trying to please everyone and gets treated as 'fence-sitting'. Analyse all available data and take a position based on the evidence. When new evidence comes to light, consider it, discuss it, and subsume it into your previous considerations.

Apophasis

Denying you're bringing up a subject when you are

A clear example of this would be saying, "I would never call you fat", obviously stating the thing you wish to say while pretending you do not have the intent to say it. Other examples include, "I promised I wouldn't bring up your alcoholism and I haven't" and "Why would they insult me like that? I would never call them dumb and lazy!" Note that such comments are not intended to come off as sarcasm, but rather an attempt to flatter oneself into a position of fake dignity while attempting an Ad Hominem attack. Not only is Apophasis denial, but it is also suggesting in some cases that a topic shouldn't even be brought up while bringing it up. "I shouldn't say this, but the birthday cake that your mum made was horrible" is an example of this. To respond, ask them immediately if they intended to bring up the issue, while attempting to absolve them of responsibility for saying it. Ask why they chose to do this, rather than addressing the topic at hand.

Special Pleading

Making an exemption for yourself but not others

Extremely common with theists, making a rule for everyone else that you don't have to abide by is a cheap way of wriggling out of a discussion. It usually comes up when a theist declares a general rule to be applied to everyone. When challenged, they quickly backtrack and make up an excuse as to why it does not apply to them. An example of this would be stating, "Morality comes from the Bible". When challenged on ideas like slavery - justified in Exodus - they will either defend the claim and defend slavery or claim an exemption to uphold the previous position they stated. The proper thing to do would be to retract their initial statement. This is not to say legitimate exceptions do not exist. Instead, they cannot be applied to the specific context of the discussion you are having. Always question why exemptions to the rule are being made, especially in *their* favour, and ask whether it is permissible to make exemptions for your arguments as well.

Halo Effect

You judge an idea depending on how much you like the speaker

Incredibly tricky to dislodge, the Halo Effect is dependent on our first impressions of an individual, and subsequent impressions made of that person. Most obviously deployed when said person makes a mistake, they are often held to a lower standard of critique than others around them. Someone wearing the halo will more often than not be given the benefit of the doubt. Either everyone is treated equally, or nobody is. Essentially, Special Pleading is making an exemption for yourself, but the Halo Effect is justifying an exemption for others. Commonly deployed towards romantic interests, we must be careful in identifying where our biases lie. Cult leaders also tend to be treated as though they are incapable of doing wrong. Often, they do a significant amount of damage when taking advantage of their loyal subjects. Try to criticise everyone equally, especially yourself, and those you are more attracted to.

Texas Sharpshooter

Identifying a pattern to fit your pre-existing opinion

A specific form of Cherry Picking, this is more to do with identifying patterns in data to match existing beliefs. The name comes from the idea that a cowboy in Texas fires their gun randomly at a barn door. The cowboy notices that some of the shots are close together. Around those shots, the cowboy paints an archery-style target, claiming to have aimed at it perfectly from the beginning. They go on to ignore all of the surrounding bullet holes that were nowhere near the newly painted target. Theists will use this to prove a prophecy from their holy book. Let's say this book makes 10 prophecies, and 1 of them comes true. I dismiss the other 9 predictions in a future edition of the book and pretend I only made 1 prophecy from the beginning, citing how amazing I am at predicting the future. It can be tricky to notice, but a sharpshooter will convince others to make Hasty Generalisations about a small data set. Do your due diligence and evaluate all of the available data.

Appeal to Motive

Dismissing a claim due to questionable incentives

Questioning someone's intent is perfectly normal. The issue is when we use these suspicions to reject the claim being proposed. Someone could claim something entirely rational, only for it to be ridiculed or ignored. An example of this would be the accusation that anyone promoting the idea of man-made Climate Change is a shill, with vested interests. Are those that deny the existence of aliens being paid by NASA to cover up the truth? The accusation that 'you only say you're not a Christian because you want to sin' is an easy way to get out of trying to understand an atheist's position. Start by trying to find out what makes them think those motives are there, and then identify where the evidence for that comes from. They likely have a legitimate concern that ought to be taken seriously. Do your best to not be offended by their accusation and, as best as possible, work towards an understanding of what each other's position is.

The Fallacy Fallacy

Assuming a conclusion is wrong because a fallacy was used to justify it

Lastly, this is probably the most crucial fallacy of the lot - one that you may have been using without realising throughout reading this book. Just because someone justified their opinion using a fallacy does not mean that their conclusion is wrong. It just means that they gave you a bad reason, maybe because they put too much emphasis on who told them. If a Theist claims they believe in God because their friend had a vision in a dream, this is an Anecdotal Fallacy. However, the proper course of action would be to point this out to the user. Ask for subsequent evidence of the claim, rather than to outright dismiss the claim because a fallacy was used. This is why I claim I will be an atheist up until a proper syllogism can be structured to support the existence of God. One has not yet been found...

You now have a rudimentary understanding of some of the most common logical fallacies. This list is not exhaustive and will be added to with a follow-up series of literature. Remember Rapoport's Rules:

1. Repeat their position back to them accurately
2. State what you agree on
3. State anything that you have learned
4. Respectfully criticise the argument

It's tricky to follow all the time, so work your way towards maximising your use of these rules in ordinary conversations, while minimising your use of the fallacies in question.

Note, you are well-advised to allow others to borrow this book, especially if your Pastor wishes to burn it. It will give the book excellent exposure, as sales and popularity will likely soar.

I wish you all the very best with the conversations that lie ahead of you.

David Robert Worley was born in Hayes, West London. After a couple of summers working in America, he took to the online atheist community to start the worleyDR Podcast. David continues to interview a wide range of personalities from Secular and Futurist backgrounds, providing escapism for those who dare to think for themselves. To help make the online sceptic community go full-time, consider supporting us on Patreon or PayPal.

A thank you to all my Patrons who continue to allow me to do the work I do.

Activism requires time, time typically spent working a full-time job.

It is vitally important that we, the content creators, get the chance to spend as much time as possible helping others with our content.

To do this, we rely on donations from people like you to keep the lights on.

If you would like to become a Patron for as little as $1 a month, please visit:

www.patreon.com/davidworley

Contacts and Social Media

YouTube – David Worley

Website - www.worleydr.com/

Patreon - www.patreon.com/davidworley

PayPal – www.paypal.me/worleyDR

Merch – www.davidworley.teemill.com

Twitter - @worleyDR

Insta - worleydr

Discord - discord.gg/RnnsCBf

FB - www.facebook.com/worleyDRPodcast

A final thanks to my proof readers, for without them, I would have made many mistakes in this book. You know who you are :)

Printed in Great Britain
by Amazon